UNDERSTANDING THE BASICS OF E-PUBLISHING

UZOAMAKA OGWO

ISBN: 9798715184337

Cover design by: Art Painter
Library of Congress Control Number: 2018675309
Printed in the United States of America

This work is dedicated to the Almighty God, for His faithfulness, protection, provisions and sustenance throughout the period of this work. He is the source of my wisdom and strength.

CONTENTS

FOREWORD

In spite of the many information materials on e-publishing, there is always room for more and current information, especially when such is targeted towards a very important skill acquisition that will enable users to be to independent e-publishers.

This book is an introductory note on E-Publishing training. This comprises both the notes for basic and Master's training lectures. This centres on the fundamental skills and information on E-book publishing on Amazon. This lecture note will serve as an invaluable training resource on E-book publishing on Amazon. The lecture note covers the basic information on the concept of writing and what makes a strong writing and bestsellers. It also gives an introductory note on E-book publishing. Formatting e-book using Creatspace is also covered.

The author, Dr. Uzoamaka Ogwo is an experienced writer and this piece of work is aimed at familiarizing users with e-publishing skills on Amazon platform.

PREFACE

The primary aim of this book is to bring to lime light, the basic principles of e-publishing on Amazon platform. This book provides the fundamental information and skills on E-publishing.

In the contemporary digital environment, e-publishing skill has become very necessary for scholars, students, lectures and anyone who may engage in the act of writing. This is as a result of preference given to electronic materials in the contemporary age.

This work is designed and organized in such a way that it provides the users with the background information and skills required for e-publishing on Amazon platform. It provides the basic concepts of writing, formatting and ePublishing.

UNDERSTANDING THE BASICS OF E-PUBLISHING

UZOAMAKA OGWO

ISBN: 9798715184337

DEDICATION

This work is dedicated to the Almighty God, for His faithfulness, protection, provisions and sustenance throughout the period of this work. He is the source of my wisdom and strength.

ACKNOWLEDGEMENTS

The researcher wishes to express her sincere appreciation to a number of persons who contributed immensely to the successful completion of this training. The researcher is grateful to her coach, Mr. Solomon Okpa for impacting a lot of skills on her on e-publishing.

The author also wants acknowledge Dr. Ijeoma Ibegbulem and Miss Bukola James for inviting her for this training programme and for their guidance throughout the training programme.

PREFACE

The primary aim of this book is to bring to lime light, the basic principles of e-publishing on Amazon platform. This book provides the fundamental information and skills on E-publishing.

In the contemporary digital environment, e-publishing skill has become very necessary for scholars, students, lectures and anyone who may engage in the act of writing. This is as a result of preference given to electronic materials in the contemporary age.

This work is designed and organized in such a way that it provides the users with the background information and skills required for e-publishing on Amazon platform. It provides the basic concepts of writing, formatting,

FORWARD

IN SPITE OF THE MANY INFORMATION MATERIALS ON E-PUBLISHING, THERE IS ALWAYS ROOM FOR MORE AND CURRENT INFORMATION, ESPECIALLY WHEN SUCH IS TARGETED TOWARDS A VERY IMPORTANT SKILL ACQUISITION THAT WILL ENABLE USERS

TO BE TO INDEPENDENT E-PUBLISHERS.

This book is an introductory note on E-Publishing training. This comprises both the notes for basic and Master's training lectures. This centres on the fundamental skills and information on E-book publishing on Amazon. This lecture note will serve as an invaluable training resource on E-book publishing on Amazon. The lecture note covers the basic information on the concept of writing and what makes a strong writing and bestsellers. It also gives an introductory note on E-book publishing. Formatting e-book using Creatspace is also covered.

The author, Dr. Uzoamaka Ogwo is an experienced writer and this piece of work is aimed at familiarizing users with e-publishing skills on Amazon platform.

THE CONCEPT OF WRITING

WHAT IS WRITING?

Writing is a medium of human communication that involves the representation of ideas, thoughts and language with symbols. Writing is done systematically. Writing fosters our ability to explain and refine our ideas to others and ourselves. In this context is an impulse to scribble one's idea, thoughts, and stories. Writing is the act of documenting ideas and experiences. Writing is an act of putting wordings, thought and idea into print. It is an act of putting creative ideas together, documentarily in certain order for others to read and be impacted.

Writing is putting down an idea, knowledge in more constructive way, to benefit both the writer and the reader, which could outlast them. It is born out of creativity. Writing is a very important skill in communication. Good writing skills allow one to communicate effectively.

In writing, it is important to refer to what others have written on the subject matter. In some cases, one may need to *paraphrase* (writing someone else's ideas and information using your own words) or *direct quotation*(writing an author's idea verbatim). In any of these ways, it is very important to make reference to the author of the work you have consulted during your writing exercise. Failure to do so, is a very serious academic offense called *Plagiarism* which means intellectual theft.

Plagiarism is the act of copying or stealing someone else's intellectual work or idea as your own without adequate citation or acknowledging the original source. Plagiarism may be intentional or unintentional. In an academic environment, plagiarism is considered as a form of intellectual theft or fraud. This unethical and dishonest practice may lead to disciplinary actions that may even lead to expulsion. Hence, plagiarism is a punishable offence as it is a form of intellectual theft.

Plagiarism is very rampant in the present digital environment where it has become so easy to copy, edit and paste other people's work without proper citation and referencing. The avalanche of information over the internet has made it easier for one to copy other peoples work without proper citation.

Plagiarism can include the following:

- ➢ Copying and pasting of information from a source without enclosing the text in a quotation mark and without giving credence to the original author.
- ➢ Paraphrasing or summarizing someone else's work or idea without acknowledgement
- ➢ Re-using a work that you have previously submitted as a fresh work. This is called self-plagiarism

WHEN TO STOP WRITING?

- When you feel like stopping
- When writing becomes a struggle.
- When you feel like increasing the content of your writing.
- When you feel like adding just anything and everything into your writing then pause.
- When you are tired or distracted.

WHAT IS STRONG WRITING?

Strong writing is a kind of writing that meets both the needs of the writer and that of the target audience. It is also writing to satisfy the needs and interest of the audience to the point that they are willing to pay for it at all cost. It can also be defined as an act of relating or communicating ideas, responding to real situations of readers through printed words.

It simply means no dull moment, where every word of a story strikes interest in the reader. Strong writing means no dull moments. It doesn't mean you have to write an action-packed story in the strictest sense of the word, but it does mean things need to happen in every chapter, and there needs to be a "hanger" at the end of each chapter that will keep your reader reading.

It helps to arouse the readers' emotion to keep reading. It also creates a strong and permanent impression in the mind of both the writer and the reader.

A strong book or writing is beyond meeting the literary needs rather it is aimed at meeting the literary needs of the target audience, to the extent that they are willing to pay for extra money to purchase a copy for themselves.

WHAT IS BEST SELLER?

Best seller with respect to books is books that have sold a great number of copies. They are books that are well written with lot of ideas that touch the life of a reader and have a great number of sales. They are popular literature without recourse to strict literary rules or morals with mass appeal been the focus. It commands reader's patronage due to the quality of its content.

When we say best seller, we are referring to a book/publication that has the highest number of sold out copies in relation to other books in its category within a given time frame. The sales can be much above 20,000 copies sold out within a specified period of time. A bestseller therefore is a book that, for a time, leads all others of its kind in sales

TIPS FOR WRITING A BEST SELLER

- Start with a big idea, bestsellers are built on a big idea
- Start immediately

- Belief that you something valuable to say.
- Write with the audience in mind. Bestsellers are sticky
- Capture the readers' attention with your opening lines
- Bookworm your way to success (cultivate the habit of reading i.e. be a reading role model)
- Be in the company of like minds (authors) show me your friends and I will tell you who you are
- Edit for clarity, not perfection
- Package your book to spread (great marketing strategy lies in good packaging)

The Five major Tips to set a book up for success so that it has a chance of becoming a bestseller include the following.

1. **Start with a big idea.**

Bestsellers are built on a big idea. Not just some old thing regurgitated in a new way. It's something fresh and interesting. Something NOVEL. You must find an idea that will get readers excited to pick up your book. This goes for fiction, nonfiction, how-to, manuscripts and memoir. A small idea for a book results in small sales. And a book idea, well, you get the picture. J.R.R. Tolkien spent years developing the languages upon which his entire world would later be built. Don't neglect the importance of nailing a big idea before you begin writing. And don't rush the research.

2. Write with the audience in mind. Bestsellers are sticky.

The book needs to be written in a way where it can be easily shared and talked about, because it touches on some universal theme. In other words, don't just write a book for yourself. Stephen King says you write the first draft with the door closed and the second draft with the door open. That's good protocol.

3. **Edit for clarity, not perfection**. Bestsellers are clear. Take out all the clutter that distracts your reader from the true message. Editing is not about making the book grammatically perfect (if

that were true, books would be typo free). Rather, it is the process of making your book into what it's supposed to be. So every time you edit your work, ask yourself, "Is this helping what I'm trying to say, or hurting it?"

4. Package your book to spread. Bestsellers are packaged to sell. The title, cover, and design are all optimized to help the message spread. The way people experience your book will affect how well the book sells and how far it spreads. Your goal is to not only get this thing into people's hands; it's to give them something they want to share. This includes the decisions you make regarding title, cover, artwork, and design etc

5. Launching is key: Never stop launching. Bestsellers are perennial. The bestselling books of all time typically didn't come out of the gates as immediate successes. But because of their timeless nature, they just kept selling. Book launches are great, but you're going to need more than one big event to sell this thing. Understanding the three unique launch phases of a book will help you sell your first 1000 or so copies, but it won't help you sell your next 10,000 or 100,000 copies. The best way to do that is to never stop launching. You just have to keep talking about it for a long time.

EXAMPLES OF BEST SELLER BOOKS

- Harry Potter
- Things Fall Apart
- Marriage of Anasewa
- Trial of Brother Jero
- Last Days at Farcado High School
- Rich Dad Poor Dad
- Best seller Authors are Ben Carson, Brian Tracy, Robert Kiyosaki, Etc.

BASIC PARTS OF A BOOK

What is a Book?

A book may additionally be described as a non-periodical printed publication of not less than forty-nine pages exclusive of cover pages. A book is a compilation of intellectual work, arranged in a systematic order on any subject matter, which has been published or printed in a bound volume with a protective cover.

The 3 major part of a book are:

Books are generally divided into three parts: The *front cover*, the *body* (intellectual part) of the book, and the *back cover*. Each part of the book contains very important and specific elements that normally appear in a specific order. The front matter are the preliminary pages of a book. They include, cover page/ title, copy right page, dedication, epigraph, prologue, acknowledgements and table of contents.

The body or the intellectual content of the book is also known as the main page of a book. It is made up of the book chapters. The back matter is the subsidiary pages of a book which includes references, bibliographies and indexes.

DIFFERENT SECTIONS OF A BOOK

The sections of a well acceptable book include:

➢ **Cover page**: This is the protective part of the book. It could be paper-back or hard-cover back. The front cover of the book bears information about the title of the book, the author's name, edition, series and sometimes illustrations. The back cover sometimes contains information about the author, background information about the book, ISBN and publishers address. Another important part of the book cover is the spine of the book that mostly bears the title of the book, the author's name and the publisher's crest.

➢ **Title Page:** Just as the name implies, the title page is the page that indicates the title of the book or the name by which the book is designated. This is a repetition of the information on the cover page. It provides the reader with the information about the book title, the author(s), the publisher, the location of the publisher and the year of publication. No book is complete without the title page. Some books may have:

Subtitle: is an explanatory phrase that further clarifies the main title. For example: Fundamentals of the Library: instructions on the use of the library and information literacy. Books that are written in more than one language have a parallel title.

Parallel title is a title, appearing in conjunction with the title proper, in another Language or script, for example, English and French. It is important to note that cataloguers rely mostly on the information on the title page during book processing.

Running Title: This is the title usually repeated at the top edge of each page showing the chapter heading. In some cases, it is italized or written in a smaller font size than the main book font size. Another name for running title is "running head".

➢ **Copy right page** also called a "colophon" and also the verso page. The copyright is found on the verso of the title page. The copyright page contains information that helps to register your book in the community and protect the intellectual property right. It is the page that gives the information about the edition of the book, the copyright notice, legal notices, publication information, printing history, cataloguing-in-publication information (CIP) data, and the International Standard Book Number (ISBN) which serves as the book's identification number. The copyright notice consists of three parts: the symbol ©, the year the book is published, and the name of the copyright owner.

- **Dedication page**: This page typically comes after the copyright page. The page is always a very short page that contains the author's appreciation and devotion message to someone who is very important to the author. It indicates the person in whose honour the book is written. It is very similar to an acknowledgements page and sometimes they are used interchangeably. Sometimes both pages exist in the same work. The dedication page is usually a more heartfelt acknowledgment of someone very special to the author.
- **Acknowledgments**: This page is where the author expresses his gratitude and appreciation to those who in one way or the other have made positive contribution to the successful completion of the book such as supervision, editing, data collection, resources, publishing, or for moral and financial support.
- **Table of content:** This is one of the preliminary page that shows the main headings and sub-headings of the chapters of a book alongside their page location. It contains the outlines of the intellectual content treated in the chapters of the book. The table of contents is like a roadmap, a guide and index that points to the pages of a book where the titles could be found. This helps for easy access and navigation of the book
- **Introduction:** This is a short essay or statement, usually being a general survey of the subject preparing the reader for the treatment to follow. It is a preliminary note, usually following the table of contents, presenting a general background to the subject of the book and discussing its treatment. It may occur as the first chapter of the book
- **Epigraph:** A phrase, quotation or poem that is set at the beginning of a document, monograph or a section of a write-up.
- **The interior (the body):** this is the main part of the book as it

contains the intellectual content of the book otherwise called the main text. It may or may not contain illustrations such as tables, pictures, maps and diagrams. It is made up of chapters, headings and subheading that addresses the main subject of the book.

- **The back matter** (the author writes to give a short description about the book (blurb) and about his/her own biography.
- **ISBN**: A unique 13-digit identifier given to a book. It is usually written at the verso of the title page. It is a unique identification number assigned to every book by an authorized national agency prior to its publication in order to identify the publisher, title, edition and volume number. It is very important as it helps in tracking the book, facilitates ordering, acquisition, cataloguing, and circulation procedures in libraries.
- **Blurb**: is also known as "about the book". This is a short description of a book that is written for promotional purposes. It is usually written at the back of a book or duct jacket that gives brief information and sometimes contains the price of the book. It may be written by the author or the publisher. The main purpose of witting a blurb is to convince a potential buyer or reader to take a chance on it.
- **Barcode**: they are found at the back cover of a book, basically at the rear after the author's biography)

E-BOOK PUBLISHING

WHAT IS EBOOK AND PAPERBACK?
E-book simply means "electronic book" or book in electronic format which is not physically handled. It is a book that is written and published through electronic media/ medium instead of hard copy or as an extension of hard copy to reach a wider audience. E-books are electronic version of printed books which can be read on a computer or other electronic and mobile devices such as smart phones, tablets, laptops etc. E-books are made available in a digital form and it consists of text, images, animations and it is readable through electronic devices. Many books that are in a hard copy version are also available in electronic version. E-books are becoming very popular especially in the present digital environment. Most e-books are freely available online and can generally be downloaded, copied and shared without restrictions.

Paper back is a book published in print form that is bound with a soft paper covering as opposed to hard cover binding. Paperback is the soft cover of a print book that can be contrast with a hard-cover.
The availability of e-books facilitate e-learning. Innovations in telecommunications and technology industry are presenting new possibilities in libraries and have transformed the way information is accessed, retrieved and disseminated. With ubiquitous availability of electronic mobile devices such as laptops, tablets,

smart phones, Wi-Fi hotspot, students can download and read e-books anytime, anywhere. This has solved the challenge of physical boundary where students must visit a physical library in order to have access to a book. Students can now read from the comfort of their home through mobile devices. Harman (2018) revealed that e-books are all-in-one device which provides a wholesome learning experience to students. Most users prefer e-books because of its multiple interactive features. Current information resources are being produced in combinations of text, graphics, video and audio sounds, animation and virtual reality.

Advantages of E-books

E-books offer substantial advantages to libraries and their users. There are some features that distinguish it from the conventional printed version of a book. These features include:

- **Easy and fast production:** it takes a little time to produce electronic books than the traditional printed version. Timeliness is an important factors as the more current the information, the more useful it is.
- **No physical boundary**. It offers the users the opportunity to access information anywhere, anytime. Users do not need to be physically present in the library before using any book of their choice and from all over the world can gain access to the same information, as long as an internet connection is available.
- **Round the clock and Simultaneous Access:** a great number of users can have 24/7 access to the same e-Book simultaneously. An electronic version of a book is easily accessible to a wider audience from virtually any electronic device that is connected to the internet. The availability of smartphones, tablets, laptops and desktops enable one to have easy access to electronic books with the availability of internet connection. Simultaneous access to up-to-date content represents one of the most important benefits of e-book.

- **Flexibility:** It is easier to update, download, copy and paste electronic version of a book. One can include links to YouTube videos, presentations and other online resources as part of your e-book.
- **Cost effectiveness:** High cost of production of hardcopy books is one of its challenges. The cost of producing e-books is relatively lower when compared to the cost of producing hardcopy books. It reduces maintenance costs of damaged books, loss, and security concerns.
- **Easy to retrieve information**: e-books have a search function that enable readers to easily navigate and search for titles, keywords or phrases in the book. Its enhanced search functionality enables users to retrieve information across specified groups of documents and across entire catalogs within seconds. The search functionality reduces time spent on each title and increases access to a greater number of titles.
- **Multiple Interactive features**: the option to request readers to provide their views, comments and feedback. Such useful information could be used to improve the content of the book subsequently. Also, e-books have some features where students can highlight texts in the book and share these highlights and notes with other students. Other important feature such as annotations, hyper linking, page zoom, search option, copy and paste, adjust font size, read aloud makes e-book more interactive
- **Multiple formats**: e-books have all kinds of multimedia which include text, sound, animation and video.
- **Easily advertised:** the possibility to reach wider audience through social media platform and websites
- **Interoperability:** so many readers can have access to the electronic version of a book simultaneously given the available devices and network connectivity
- **Printable:** the possibility to have a printed version of e-books when the need arises
- **Portability:** instead of carrying an overload of printed books, thousands of e-book can be easily accessed through smart

phones, tablets, laptops and other mobile devices.

- **Reduce Storage space in library:** e-books helps in eliminating large space that is usually occupied by physical books in libraries. Digital devices have the ability to hold thousands and millions of books in just a single mobile device.

CREATING AN EBOOK

The Creation of an eBook starts from the process of using Microsoft word to format the writer's document/manuscript. E-Book are created after thorough and proper editing that has been done on a book manuscript and are successfully uploaded online using an eBook creation / publisher software or eBook creation/publishing site. This is done or achieved after one must have duly registered with an online publishing firm. eBooks enhance wider coverage and marketability of the book.

USING A KINDLE CREATE APP TO FORMATT AND CONVERT A WORD DOCUMENT INTO AN EBOOK

FORMATTING AN EBOOK

Formatting an eBook is the process of changing the layout or visual style of a typed author's manuscript in preparation for an eBook publishing. Formatting has to do with following diligently the author's guideline for the publisher. E.g. font style, font size, line spacing etc.

WHAT IS A TEMPLATE?

A template is an accepted pattern/layout/model/guide/formula that is followed in replicating or creating things similar to it. It is a guide that is to be followed to make other things.

Template in publishing is a particular laid down pattern widely accepted, that must be followed when publishing a hard copy book or an eBook. It is a generic model or pattern used for publishing an eBook. It refers to the accepted style that guides a publisher when publishing a hard copy book or an eBook.

BASIC PRACTICAL STEPS OF FORMATTING A WORD DOCUMENT FOR CONVERSION INTO AN EBOOK

Step 1. Set your page and margin. (Trim paper size to 6"×9")
Step 2. Choose suitable styles and customize same. (Garamond font style and font size 11 is acceptable at the Amazon platform)
Step 3. Format the interiors - chapters.
Step 4. Fix your cover designates: title
Step 5. Do pagination (A minimum of 14 pages)
Step 6. Headers fixation
Step 7. Extras: footers
Step 8. add images if available
Step 9. Table of contents (toc)
Step 10. Proof-read and convert from Microsoft word (docx) to pdf.

HOW TO TRIM YOUR PAPER SIZE MANUALLY USING MS WORD

To trim to the universally accepted size of 6"×9", do the following:

- Go to home page on your MS word window
- Click on layout or page layout.
- Click on size above page set up to open dialogue box
- Click on more paper sizes to open up another dialogue box
- Adjust default paper size under letter to 6"×9" (width and length)
- Click ok

FORMATTING YOUR WORD DOCUMENT USING A CUSTOMIZED TEMPLATE

Formatting could be defined as how a manuscript looks and reads. It includes things like font size, page color, word count, page number, line spacing, paragraph breaks. It also entails everything that goes into the visual appearance in the course of writing a book. This means manuscript format is the proper way your manuscript should look when you send it in for editing. Formatting is therefore how your manuscript looks and reads. Formatting also makes information more accessible to the reader by creating and labeling sections (headings), highlighting key words or ideas (bold, italics, or lists), and making a good impression (professional look and feel, appropriate font choice for the document type).

CREATESPACE is a customized template used for formatting the visual style and layout of an eBook, published by Amazon. It provides publishers with a laid down pattern that must be followed when publishing an eBook on Amazon.

ACCOUNT CREATION

Upon manual formatting of the eBook using the basic formatting method of the Create Space template, you are required to create a KDP (Kindle Direct Publishing) account at https://kdp.amazom.com where you upload and publish your book for the whole world to see within the next 72 hours.

E-PUBLISHING AND UPLOADING OF CLASS NOTES ON AMAZON

WHAT IS E-PUBLISHING?

Electronic publishing (also referred to as publishing, digital publishing, or online publishing) includes the digital publication of e-books, digital magazines, and the development of digital libraries and catalogues. It also includes an editorial aspect, that consists of editing books, journals or magazines that are mostly destined to be read on a screen (computer, e-reader, tablet, Smartphone).

PROCEDURES FOR E-PUBLISHING ON AMAZON PLATFORM

- Sign in to your Kdp account through Amazon (/kdp.amazon.com)
- On your account page you will find the bookshelf (click on the bookshelf)
- Click on CREATE eBook or KINDLE EBOOK
- Create your cover page (either using the one you have designed or get a cover page from the gallery)
- Proceed to the content (Remember that you must have trimmed your paper size to 6" by 9") click on bleeds if it a pdf file. Bleeds is used for publishing a portable docu-

ment file (pdf) only. It helps to remove white borders from images and pictures when the standard trimmed page size top and bottom size margins were not used. Once you click on bleed, all pages of the book are adjusted to remove white borders at the edges.

- Click on upload to upload your manuscript (the system will automatically upload this manuscript and when it has fully uploaded it will preview)
- Scroll through in the preview pane to confirm that everything is okay
- Click on publish once you have ascertained that you are satisfied.
- After the upload your paper will come live in 2-3 days (72hours).

USING AMAZON KINDLE CREATE APP TO FORMAT AND CONVERT A WORD DOCUMENT INTO AN EBOOK.

Kindle Create is a free interior formatting tool that works well with most books you want to publish on Amazon, but there are requirements and supported features we want you to know about before you download. The Amazon kindle create app, is an app developed by Amazon to help publishers format typed manuscript into an acceptable EBook standard on Amazon. Kindle Create helps you format your Kindle ebook. If you are self-publishing Kindle ebooks on Amazon Kindle Direct Publishing (KDP)

BASIC STEPS TO FOLLOW WHEN FORMATTING A TYPED MANUSCRIPT ON KINDLE CREATE APP

1. After typing the document on Ms Word, do not format! i.e. don't include the front or back matter.
2. Download and open the kindle create app on your pc.
3. Wait for the kindle create app to load. It will take you to the main menu where you have "create new", "choose from existing file" "choose file from your computer".
4. select as appropriate and click on open to load the file and import it for formatting on the kindle create App.

COVER CREATION USING THE COVER CREATOR TOOL

The cover tool helps to automatically create a cover for every Ebook uploaded on Amazon. It saves the stress of having to create the Ebook cover manually and uploading it online.

To use the cover creation tool, one must have successfully uploaded his/ her ebook on the Kdp online. The cover tool is made up of cover designs and styles for an ebook cover.

GUIDE TO PAPERBACK COVER CREATION

The cover tool helps to automatically create a cover for every paperback uploaded on Amazon. It saves the stress of having to create the Ebook paperback cover manually and uploading it online.

To use the cover creation tool, one must have successfully uploaded his/ her ebook paper back on the Kdp online. The cover tool is made up of cover designs, fonts and styles for an ebook cover.

References

Amazon Kindle Create App. https://www.google.com/search?ei=dzo9YIHhGZCq5wLE0bxw&q=uses+of+amazon+kindle+create+app&oq=uses+of+amazon+kindle+create

+app&gs_lcp=Cgdnd3Mtd2l6EAM6BwgAEEcQsANQ9ZAKW-MOrCmDNtQpoAXACeAGAAc8FiAGKMJIBB-TUtOC4ymAEAoAEBqgEHZ3dzLXdpesgBCMABAQ&sclient=gws-wiz&ved=0ahUKEwjB-IKr5I_vAhUQ1VkKHcQoDw4Q4dUDCA0&uact=5

"E-publishing". *MaRS*. Retrieved July 13, 2018. https://en.wikipedia.org/wiki/Electronic_publishing

Harman, M. (2018). Importance of e-books in education. https://kitaboo.com/importance-of-ebooks-in-education/

www.ingramcontent.com/pod-product-compliance
Lightning Source LLC
LaVergne TN
LVHW052109160826
845678LV00015B/3454

* 9 7 9 8 7 1 5 1 8 4 3 3 7 *